A Gift of Love

Pamala Barber

ISBN 979-8-88685-133-5 (paperback)
ISBN 979-8-88685-134-2 (digital)

Christian Faith Publishing, Inc.
832 Park Avenue
Meadville, PA 16335
www.christianfaithpublishing.com

Printed in the United States of America

To my readers. I hope that you have had at least half as much fun reading my e-book as I had writing it.

To my family: Thank you all for your confidence, encouragement, love, and support.

I love writing what's in my heart and have a passion to encourage people. Being a positive influence is a good way to uplift those who need a helping hand. I want to be the difference.

- It all started with sending messages to my friends on the phone.
- Then I decided to do a blog to reach more people.
- And now, another chapter in my life—my first e-book.

Thank you for going on this exciting journey with me.

Love,
Pamala

CONTENTS

INTRODUCTION

What started to be a wonderful idea is now my first e-book. The writing was the easy part. I was having so much fun writing what was in my heart I didn't and still don't want to stop. I have such a passion for writing.

I want my readers to know that I care and want to help them feel better about themselves. We are in these trying times together. You are not alone.

The messages I write are fun, positive, inspirational, and uplifting. It is my true desire that every person who reads my e-book feels loved and inspired.

1

A Thankful Heart

Writing makes me happy. It's my way of expressing what's on my mind and in my heart. This is my first e-book. I want it to be fun, inspirational, uplifting, and entertaining. We need some joy and positivity in these trying times. Let's focus on being happy.

Enjoy life to the fullest. Today, do something that makes you happy. If we're happy today, tomorrow will be so much easier. We will get through these tough times together. Remember that song around 1988, "Don't Worry, Be Happy"? Today, let's spread happiness and cheer. Make someone smile and say, "Hi," to a complete stranger. That could make their day because you acknowledged them. It's nice to let people know they are not lost and forgotten in the shuffle. That's what we do.

Little acts of kindness *matter*. A gentle reminder that things don't have to be grand or perfect to be what we really need. Life is complicated enough. Focus on the good and positive. What we do to uplift people is a *good* thing. Reading our scriptures is a *better* thing. Knowing our heavenly Father loves us is the *best* thing.

Whether we realize it or not, our actions make an impact on more than ourselves. Being mindful of that can help us become more *Christlike*. It's all a learning process. Christ is our best teacher. His handbook would be His scriptures. He wants us all to succeed with glory and righteousness. Be willing to act with kindness. Act because it's the right thing to do. Life is full of unexpected surprises. Being kind shouldn't be one of them. Being kind should be second nature for us. All these little gestures are really big to one of God's children. Always keep that in mind.

Celebrate the joys of life and praise the One who sends them.

2

My Wheels Are Turning

Sometimes I feel the more I have going on the better I do. I wonder if that is really true. My focus is on so many wonderful thoughts and ideas. I guess it would be nice to narrow them down and prioritize. Look, I figured out what I needed to do. Now is the real challenge. Everything is important to me. Where do I begin?

A Ferris wheel comes to mind when I think of all the inspiring, mind-blowing excitement I feel when my thoughts and ideas start flowing. I want to share everything, but I know I have to have some control. So as the carts on the Ferris wheel start filling up, I have to start throwing thoughts and brilliant ideas out that keep occurring to me. I'll save them for the next Ferris wheel that comes along.

So buckle up, buttercup, and enjoy life's journey. Life is full of unexpected twists and turns as we are all aware of; some are much more surprising than others. As long as we keep our sense of humor, positive attitude, and delightful spirit, we can conquer anything.

Writing lets me do just that—it makes me happy and is my way to share and reach out. I am now retired, and I wondered, *Hmm, what now?* I've always had a desire to write, I love scrapbooking, I enjoy doing service projects and helping people, I'm not an idle person. My decision was easy. I can do it all! Life is too short to sit and do nothing. Do what you enjoy and makes you happy.

Whatever it is, pick one thing and make it happen. We are all unique, just like God wants us. He wants us to be happy and filled with the desire to act. Make a commitment to do one nice thing out of the ordinary every day for yourself or someone you've been thinking about. There is so much around us to be inspired and hopeful about.

There is no doubt sadness and dismay are around us. If we look with an open heart and Christlike eyes, we can see so much beauty and potential. Let us focus on the positive and uplifting.

There is a lot of good we miss because we are bombarded with the bad, evil, and negativity. If we could change one thing to a positive, what would we work on changing?

For me, I would like to have more patience with things I don't understand. Sometimes, the human side of me is quick to judge. My Christlike side says, "Pamala, my child, what have you been taught? The Lord loves us unconditionally, even when we fall short. He knows we know what to do, but as a child of God, He has to gently remind us."

The Lord loves us unconditionally, even when we fall short. He knows we know what to do. Even being a child of God, He has to gently remind us.

*"Let us not become weary in doing good, for at
the proper Time we will reap a harvest if we do not
give up" (Galatians 6:9 NIV).*

3

Excuses Hold Us Back

Did you know that excuses multiply like little bunnies, but they are not as cute and definitely don't bring us joy? Excuses hold us back from what we're trying to accomplish. They keep us in the dark and don't want us to be happy and see the light. We need to wake up and acknowledge if it's a just reason or an excuse. We are all guilty at one time or another. Sometimes it's easier not to do something and try to justify it with a creative excuse.

And, oh dear, are there some creative excuses. For instance: my schedule is so busy, I can't do one more thing. I have a headache or I didn't make it to church because I didn't have anything to wear. The excuses are endless. *No excuses*! We all know if it's something we really want to do, we would make time, and we would get it done. Could it be procrastination? I'll do it when I can fit it in my busy schedule. When will that be? Meanwhile, someone is counting on us, and we are letting them down because we are too busy!

Somehow that sounds kind of selfish. Don't you agree? This has been on my mind. How many times have I let someone down because I was too busy? That definitely has to change. People must come first. Things can wait a little longer. I want to do what I do with a true sincerity of heart. Excuses, ignoring promptings are kind of in the same category.

We don't get random promptings. They are specifically designed for us individually. By listening for and acting on promptings, we become closer to God because we are His children. That's a blessing in itself. What are your blessings? To me, looking around where I am at in my life is a blessing. Having a church family that makes me feel like I belong is a blessing.

Being outside in the cool fresh air and seeing the wonderment of nature makes me smile; it's a blessing. Knowing I have a loving husband of thirty-nine years who is supportive and loves me for who I am is a true blessing. Our blessings are tailor-made just for us. Think outside the box and use your talents to help someone who is struggling and just needs a helping hand.

Bless someone with kindness because it's the right thing to do. Follow your heart and ask the Lord how He wants you to help this person. Now listen with real intent: We are all children of God and deserve hope, love, and compassion. Look, listen, and act on promptings that come our way and remember they were sent to us on purpose.

"Take delight *in the Lord and He will give*
you your heart's desires" (Psalm 37:4 NLT).

4

Never Too Old

To me, age is just a number. I don't consider myself old. I just consider myself not as young as I used to be. When I was younger, I didn't think much about the future. Now the future is here, and, wow, what did I miss? Whew, time sure flies when you're having fun. Okay, let's be honest, it wasn't all fun and games. Life happened, and I dealt with it the best I knew how.

The important thing is I never gave up. Growing up in an alcoholic household was very traumatic. Sometimes we didn't have food, but there was always beer in the house. I thought we were the only dysfunctional family on the block. Even so, I still felt embarrassed and ashamed. We were always looked at as the kids nobody wanted their kids to play with because of our home situation.

Being kids, we didn't understand. It was out of our control. To make a long story short, we somehow survived childhood and moved on. I retired from working twenty years with the State of California. My husband, Bill, and I have been married for thirty-nine years. He is the best, so loving and supportive. We have four grown children, one grandson, and two dogs, Buddy and Rocket.

My newest addition to the family is a blog that I started to spread uplifting messages, which I'm so excited about. I knew in my heart this blog is something I needed to do. Thinking of my past, I've realized what I've accomplished. I'm not telling you this to feel sorry for me. There is hope. I'm telling you this because this is a success story. I am happy and blessed, and all of my trials made me realize who I am.

I am a child of God. I am doing what I love, helping others with love and encouragement through my blog. God saw good in me and got me where I am today. I know I couldn't have made it without Him. I am so thankful. Even if I didn't realize it at the time, He was with me throughout my whole journey. My book is my way of letting you know God is good and loves us all.

Don't let your trials and life's challenges get the best of you. You are an amazing, beautiful, and brave person. Things will get better. We all have things in our lives that keep us on our toes. It's like being on the tennis court. Oh look, here comes another one. We handle that situation getting ready for the next. If we look around us with an open heart and Christlike eyes, we can see so much beauty.

There's so much potential in our surroundings. Let us focus on the positive and uplifting. There are a lot of good things we miss because we are bombarded with negativity. Let us be the change by looking at things differently. Hopefully, that will cause us to act differently with a new perspective.

Hope is a seed God plants in our hearts to
remind us there are better things ahead.

—Holley Gerth

5

A Forgotten Box

The year was 2021. We had moved in May to Spokane, Washington. Sometime right after Thanksgiving, the weather was cool with freshly fallen snow. It was a beautiful treat. Coming from Bakersfield, California, we didn't see much (any) snow. This was breathtaking. The snow delicately covered everything it touched. What a sight.

It was time to start decorating for Christmas. I love all the hustle and bustle, the beautiful colors, and fun music. Decorating for the holidays is such an enjoyment for me. This is an older house, but it's new to us. It has so much character and charm. I do have quite a few boxes, boxes, and more boxes. Good thing I love a good challenge and have a fun sense of humor.

This time of year, I'm going to need both (chuckle, chuckle). It takes a few days to put my pretty decorations all over the house. I have many different themes I like to incorporate. Somehow, we managed to get the boxes, boxes, and boxes into the house from the detached garage. We had an awesome group of youth from the church to help. My husband, Bill, directed box traffic.

Now the boxes are all in designated staging areas ready for the magic to begin. I started pulling out treasures one by one, strategically placing them where they needed to go to make a beautiful scene. As the boxes are emptied and a pile accumulates, we take them back to the garage. Slowly but surely, we see progress. The only pressure I have now is what I'm putting on myself.

Even though there were many boxes still to unpack, I feel there was one missing. I kept unpacking, hoping to find what I'm not even sure I'm missing. In the meantime, I'm listening to Christmas music as I merrily danced around to "Rocking Around the Christmas Tree." Now I'm really in the Christmas spirit. As my husband walks through the room to the kitchen, I just had to ask if he wanted to dance or help. He just smiled and moved along. Actually, I would have been shocked if the answer was anything else.

Then it dawned on me. My Christmas ties! That's what I was missing. So, now, I'm frantically looking for a box. Why is this box so important all of a sudden? Now I really have to find this box. I've been diligently working on getting all the decorations out in a timely manner. Not that it mattered to anyone but me.

A few days later and it's done. Ta-da! I have a magnificent snow village, a Coca-Cola theme, Santa Claus theme, nativity, angel theme, a bear theme, many small trees, musicals, and fun decorations galore. This was all an accumulation of many years. It didn't appear overnight. Somehow, when this project is complete, it always looks amazing. It's a lot of work but oh so worth it.

Now back to the missing box. Looking around the garage, there were many boxes neatly on shelves. Which one could it be? I pulled down several, hoping for the best. Nope, not this one or this one. The next few boxes had a few Christmas items. Still no Christmas ties. We took those in and found places to put them. How pretty. Now back to the garage we go.

Like I mentioned earlier, we recently moved, so we still had unpacked moving boxes. By this time, I'm determined to find this box. The desire is getting stronger, but why? I glanced at a box that caught my eye. I opened it, and what did I see? My Christmas ties. Finally. I thought there might be other holiday items in the same box. I got it into the house and placed it on the table.

I excitedly went through the box and saw another box. I curiously opened it. There was a smaller box that had my wedding ring in it. Oh, my goodness. I held the box and took the ring out and started to cry. They were tears of joy. I was so happy. I ran and hugged Bill as I showed him the ring I thought was lost and gone forever. My hands had gotten deformed with Dupuytren's, and I couldn't wear my wedding ring.

My husband Bill put it on a chain so I could still wear it. At the time, I put it in the box for safekeeping. It's been there for years. In the box, there were also accomplishments and awards I had received. There was also a baggie full of treasures the kids had given, me through the years, a box from the past that really makes me appreciate who I am today.

The prompting wasn't about the Christmas ties at all. If it wasn't for the ties, I wouldn't have found the real treasure. I love to sit back and enjoy the beautiful scenery. I enjoy seeing the expressions of all who visit my "Christmas Wonderland." And, yes, it is the most wonderful time of year!

6

A Touch of Inspiration

I can't help but to smile as I look out the window and see the birds fluttering from branch to branch so gracefully. The happiness I feel is so amazing as I observe the pure wonders the Lord has given us to enjoy. Does it ever cross our minds how fortunate we are in such trying times to have a heavenly Father who loves us so much? He is so good to us. He wants us to be happy and reach our full potential. He has a perfect plan and knows what we are capable of. Do we?

Sometimes, we settle for much less than we are capable of achieving. At times, it is necessary to push our limits and have more faith in God. In our hearts, we know God would never ask something of us that we could not accomplish, not to say it's always going to be easy. We are such creatures of habit and like being in our comfort zones. It's time to step up our faith, get out of our comfort zones, and see what God has in store for us.

Now is the perfect time to rejuvenate our faith. Out with the negative thinking, now in with a healthy positive approach. Don't focus on our weaknesses and insecurities, focus on being strong and courageous. Let go, let God. It's not a new concept, just one we need to be reminded of from time to time.

I just read this wonderful book by Joel Osteen, *Scriptures and Meditations for Your Best Life Now*. It says, "When God puts a dream in your heart, when he brings opportunities across your path, step out boldly in faith, expect the best, move forward with confidence, knowing that you are well able to do what God wants you to do." I just love that.

Allow yourself personal time with your Savior. Most of all, enjoy life and whatever is important to you. May this year be filled with love and compassion. Sharing my thoughts with you makes me happy. We can all take at least a few minutes out of our busy schedules to appreciate what our heavenly Father has given us to enjoy. He wants us to smile, be happy, and become more aware of our amazing surroundings.

Spokane is a very charming place to live. My husband, Bill, and I went on a fun day trip. We just drove and enjoyed the scenery. It was raining on and off all day. It was kind of fun because it was out of the ordinary. Driving around, seeing interesting yard ideas really gets my creative juices flowing. We went to Newman Lake and just enjoyed the tranquil ambiance.

It fascinates me how God puts all this for our enjoyment to make us happy and smile. When we are happy and we smile, I'm hoping He smiles also.

God has you in the right place for the right
time, for the right purpose.

7

A Marvelous Message

The new year has begun and is off to a great start. Happiness is in the air. What a wonderful time to be thankful. The holidays are now over, and we can focus on spring, which is right around the corner. I enjoy going on morning walks when the air is brisk and refreshing. It's fun to see the squirrels scurrying to get where they are going and watching the birds flutter from branch to branch.

Morning walks are a great way to relax and get ready to approach the day. My creative thoughts and ideas are flowing and waiting to be put on to paper. By the time I get home, I have a pretty good idea what topics are going to be addressed. Now is an awesome time to begin looking for new signs of life. The bare trees are getting small buds of greenery. Watching the little seedlings start growing into beautiful colorful flowers is an amazing sight to observe. Our flag is dancing to the rhythm of the tranquil cool breeze.

We grow as we endure life's trials and challenges. As we handle what life throws at us, we become stronger. As we become stronger, we learn and understand a little more.

It's so nice to hear the birds chirping. Smelling the fresh air after a gentle falling rain is so calming. Our hearts are happy to see all the beauty that surrounds us daily. You can always count on spring to bring us such joy. Little seedlings are starting to peek through. Projects we want to work on as soon as weather permits. We are getting anxious. We have a vision of what we want the outcome to look like when we are done.

God looks at us kind of like we look at spring. He sees so much potential and beauty in us. Our hearts are not only happy, they are thankful. We are like those little seedlings that need to grow and stand proud. I get so excited with my abundance of wonderful ideas and projects I like to accomplish.

Nobody in my household shares my enthusiasm! That's okay. I love a challenge. That won't stop me from doing what I enjoy. I enjoy being out in the fresh air, planting, raking, sweeping, and just general yard work. After I'm finished for the day, it's nice to step back and look at what's been accomplished. It looks good. I want it to be better. My goal is the best.

So I keep trying till I get it right. Sound familiar? Being Christlike takes a lot of effort. It's a process that's never ending. We hear the same thing over and over. Why do you think that is? The scriptures don't lie. We believe in a God we can't see, but we see Him in those around us. We can't see faith, but we know we have it. Nurturing others is well worth the effort.

We all have testimonies of the God we can't see, of the faith we know is there, and the charity that is within all of us. Nurturing ourself is well worth the effort. We are good now, and we'll work on getting better. With God's help along the way, we will be our best. Let's spring up and get to work. We can work on our yards and ourselves and make them both beautiful.

"I have come so that they may have *life* and
have it in abundance" (John 10:10 CSB).

8

Oh, My Goodness

The first thing I saw looking out the window this morning was beautiful snow gently falling, covering anything it touched. The snow is so elegant to watch as it falls. All of a sudden, the wind kicked up, and the snow appeared to be confused. It was blowing in many different directions. As breathtaking as it was to see, I felt sad and uneasy. I thought of us, God's children. We are so trusting. Sometimes, things appear to be so attractive and innocent. We let our guard down and get swept up in the confusion. Life is challenging enough without adding more confusion to the mix. Knowing who we are and what we stand for will help us make the right choices.

Are we going to occasionally make mistakes? Of course we are. Does that need to define who we are? Of course not! When we do make mistakes, that's when repentance and prayer is vital. Learning from our mistakes and not repeating them, we'll be heading in the right direction. Always remember that you have a heavenly Father and people in your life who love you and want you to succeed. We have a purpose to shine our light and be a beacon of hope.

We want others to see our light and wonder, *Hmm, I want that.* The more people that shine in these trying times will be an awesome domino effect of beauty. It can happen with a genuine effort from all of us. We all have something to offer to make our world a better place. Do a random act of kindness every day and let your light shine.

> *"For I know the plans I have for you," says the Lord. "They are for good. To give you a future and a hope" (Jeremiah 29:11 NLT).*

9

A New Chapter

We're always on a mission to do something. I think, sometimes, we feel like we're on a hamster wheel. We either can't or won't get off to try anything different from what we have been doing for so long. Actually, now is the perfect time to get off our wheel and make a change, a change for the better.

Change can be good. When you start your day, what's the first thing that goes through your mind? Is it something you want to change? Is it something you're tired of looking at? Those are such personal questions. All our answers are as unique and special as we are. There are no right or wrong answers. They are choices. If we want to improve something, we have to put forth a genuine effort to make it change.

What is important to us? Let's really focus and be honest with ourselves. A new chapter in our lives and a fresh start—wow, where do I sign? I personally have a list of things I can improve on. I guess I have to get off my wheel to get started.

- Make my list.
- Prioritize.
- Check off when completed.

Let's commit to make some changes happen. Our heavenly Father always wants us to improve and move forward. Don't look to your past. We're not going that way. Always remember who you are. We are God's children. If we listen, we will *hear Him.* Read our scriptures, listen, and act on promptings from the Holy Ghost who will help us. He has given us such a wonderful example to emulate.

Sometimes, we have a tendency to overlook the obvious. We don't need more. We need to take care of what we have. If we don't take care of our belongings, they will fall apart. If we don't give our spiritual self the attention it deserves, we will fall apart. Do you see where I'm going with this? As you continue to change, you will become stronger and even more amazing than you already are.

The result will be life-changing and well worth the effort. Do this for you and nobody else. It's not a race, it's a personal journey that we're all working on at our own pace. God is with us no matter what. That in itself should bring us comfort and peace.

Hope is a seed God plants in our hearts to
remind us there are better things ahead.

—Holly Gerth

10

Taking a Rocket for a Walk

Have you ever tried to lasso a rocket? Me neither until we inherited this cute little dog. He's a Chihuahua-schnauzer mix. Oh, what a joy he is to our family. He's full of energy and life. I'm not a big animal fan, but I do love him. I water, feed, put toys away, clean up after, and walk him. He kind of grows on you. He appears to have more in common with Bill, my husband.

During the day, he'll jump up on Bill's lap. Bill reads until he falls asleep. Read, sleep, repeat. Occasionally, Rocket will get a toy and bring it on the recliner to play tug-of-war. It's got to be exhausting to be so cute and playful. Ever since he was a puppy, he reminded me of a baby kangaroo, always jumping on his little hind legs. It appears he's spring-loaded.

The weather is cool, and the trees are bare. Clouds of off-white and gray are covering the sky. Touches of greenery are beginning to show. I needed a break from my daily typing routine. I thought a walk with Rocket would be perfect for both of us. I go to get his leash, and it all begins. He hears me and gets on his back legs, hopping like a bunny and jumping like a kangaroo.

I ask him if he wants to go for a walk. By his enthusiasm, I'd say yes! I barely get him hooked up before he heads for the door. Here we go off and running, literally. He's such an eager fella. As we head down the street, we encounter a squirrel scurrying across the street.

We greet a neighbor getting out of his car. Naturally, there was curiosity that had to be checked out. We continued down the road. He marked almost every tree in sight. I was wondering, *How much does his little bladder hold?* I was beginning to wonder, *Who's walking who?*

Soon, all the bare trees and bushes will be covered in shades of green. The empty yards will be full of beauty and color. And the birds will be enjoying the bird feeders filled with their favorite treats.

Rocket and I thank you for going on a morning walk with us. The walk was refreshing. The creative side of me is flowing with thoughts and wonderful ideas. Break time is over, let the day begin. What a wonderful way to start the day.

11

You Are Loved

Loving others is so much easier than loving ourselves. We have to *work* on that with patience and prayer. It is a *process.* We have to *learn* to love ourselves, forgive ourselves, and be kind to ourselves. How do we do that? And where do we begin? There are a few things we need to do in little increments that will add up and make a big difference.

- For starters, don't compare yourself to others. Only compare yourself to your yesterday self, you versus you. Look back long enough to see where you don't want to be, then move forward with self-improvement in mind. We all deserve to be happy. Remember, comparison is the thief of all joy.
- Second, it's not going to happen overnight. Be patient with yourself and your progress. Like a parent watching our little ones grow, we know they are going to fall. When they do, we gently pick them up so they will get stronger and fall less. Sometimes, they are going to really get hurt. Growing pains are part of life. We are all going to fall. That's okay as long as we get up and keep trying.
- And third, do all you can do to be a better you. Some ideas: read your scriptures more often with real intent; exercise a little every day, walk, use stairs; work on healthier eat-

ing habits; keep your mind sharp, puzzles, word searches, counting change back.

It's our way of letting God know we love Him. Wouldn't it be nice if life came with a manual? It does, the Word of God.

As we read and look for answers, we have to have an open heart and clear mind. We must be willing to accept the counsel given and act upon it. You are a child of a God who loves you unconditionally.

> "You must love the Lord your God with all your heart, all your soul, and all your mind. This is the first and greatest commandment" (Matthew 22:37 NLT).

12

A Day to Be Thankful

Looking out the window makes me happy. I get excited to get up and start my day. I know, you're probably wondering why is Pamala so full of energy and most of the time a happy bubbly person? It's easy. I love my life and am so thankful for all the Lord has given me. Has my life always been ideal or perfect? Not in the slightest. Most of the time, my life was like an intense roller-coaster ride.

My life has been blessed in so many ways. I try to think positive and do acts of kindness on a regular basis. Every day, there is something to remind us of God's love for us. It can be as sweet as a friend you haven't seen for a while or one of your children, out of the blue, says, "I love you, Mom."

Looking out the window to see the squirrels scurrying about is such a treat. These are things that make us smile. Our God wants us to be happy and feel His love. How has God's love touched you today?

We show Him we love Him by including Him in our daily routine. That makes Him smile, I'm pretty sure. Take a quiet moment to have a friendly conversation to express your gratitude of the many blessings you have in your life.

I *know* the course of my journey was extremely difficult until I realized what I was missing. I didn't think I was a bad person, just lost and confused. Now I make better choices.

Do I *have* to go to church? Of course not. I go because I want to go. Do I have to obey the commandments? Nope, I obey them because I *want* to, and it is a commandment given to us. These are all personal choices. I choose to follow the Savior.

What about you? Let your spirituality flow in a positive direction. Feel good about making the right choices. The Lord is on our side and will help when we open our hearts and ask.

> "Those who trust in the Lord *will find new strength.* They will soar high on wings like eagles" (Isaiah 40:31 NLT).

13

Happy Days

This is such a wonderful time to be happy. Look around and see happiness. It's all in our perspective how we see things. I prefer to see things with a positive attitude. Are negative things out there? Of course, but I sure don't want to dwell on them. I enjoy life and want to make the best of any given situation. Trust me, I've had my share of unpleasant situations. I feel I'm a lot stronger because of them. Fall down. Get up. Repeat. Never give up.

Sometimes, we feel overwhelmed. We feel like our choices don't even matter. They matter and we matter. We have to live with the decisions we make. I love this by Thomas S. Monson, "May we ever choose the harder right than the easier wrong."

There are so many positive influences to keep us moving forward:

- Our scriptures.
- Positive people in our lives.
- A good attitude.
- Listen for and acting on promptings.
- Exercise. Push ourselves to be better and healthier.

These things aren't anything new. We just need a gentle reminder from time to time. Don't look back because we're not going that way. The future is ahead, and there are so many possibilities. Starting where we are right now and focusing with a positive approach will help us get where we want to go. Is it going to be easy? Probably not. Will it be worth our effort? Absolutely!

It has a domino effect. When we're happy, those around us are happier. Circumstances don't seem quite as daunting. It appears to be a bit more peaceful, and that is calming in itself.

Today is a wonderful day. The weather is crisp, the sky is blue, and the birds are happily chirping. Most of the snow has gone. Sprouts are starting to sprout up through the moist soil. I'm anxiously waiting for temperatures to start rising so I can plant beautiful bulbs and colorful seeds. Hopefully, I'll have good luck with them.

Being outside in the fresh air makes me happy. Raking, sweeping, shoveling, and cutting is all part of the process for a prettier yard. It's nice to appreciate all of your hard work, time, and effort put into any project. The great Jamaican reggae singer, songwriter, and musician, Bob Marley, so eloquently stated, "The greatness of a man is not in how much wealth he acquires, but in his *integrity* and his ability to affect those around him positively."

Integrity

- Conduct that conforms to an accepted standard of right or wrong/having morals.
- Devotion to telling the truth/being honest.
- Faithfulness to high moral standards/having honor.

14

A Thoughtful Message

My mind has been working overtime lately, more than usual. I just want to say thank you for following my weekly blogs. This is becoming such a productive part of the new chapter in my life. I enjoy responding to your wonderful comments. This has been a good learning experience for me. My fear of technology is not going to get the best of me (ha ha).

Life is full of things we are not comfortable with. Sometimes we have to "suck it up, buttercup, and move forward." Denzel Washington is a wonderful motivational speaker. Talking to a college graduating class, he said this, "If you don't fail, you're not even trying. To get something you never had, you have to do something you never did." That is a powerful statement.

We don't know if we can do something unless we try. Think of something you've always wanted to do but been afraid to even attempt. Guess what? My blog sounded like fun. In my mind, I tried to talk myself out of doing it because I was scared of technology. Anyone I worked with would agree. Now I am so glad I tried it. I have a passion to make a difference.

Is my blog going to succeed? All I know is it's not going to fail because I didn't give it my all. My thoughts, ideas, and sense of humor will make this blog fun and heartfelt. I want to spread happiness and hope in these trying times. This is a topic full of potential. The ideas are endless. Some suggestions:

1. Walk around the block with your dog.
2. Eat carrots instead of candy (even though they both begin with *c*).
3. Take a painting class, pottery class, you get the idea.
4. Exercise with a friend.
5. Organize your pictures. Put them in photo albums.
6. Something you've always wanted to do.

Aw, the possibilities—what are some you can think of?

With spring right around the corner, let's be ready with a game plan to get motivated. It's fun and makes us feel we've accomplished something worthwhile. My thought is to uplift ourselves with a positive boost of energy.

> In the arms of God, there is strength to hold
> you, grace to sustain you, and love to carry you.

15

An Unforgettable Day Trip

It started out just like a normal day trip Bill and I was looking forward to. We wanted to check out a lake we had heard about. They had said fishing was good, and it wasn't far from home. Bill was all in. He was pretty anxious to see for himself. Before we headed to the lake, we stopped at Denny's for breakfast. The food was good, the music was fun, and the waitress was fast and efficient.

The restaurant was busy and full of hungry people. Things were moving right along. It was a pleasant atmosphere. We ate and observed families with little ones getting restless. We chuckled remembering those days. We were ready to leave when the waitress came over and said we could leave at any time. She pointed to a table and said that they paid for your meal.

It was unexpected and touching at the same time. We were thankful at the same time sad because we didn't get to thank them. Bill and I sat there for a second, kind of speechless. Bill looked around and saw two ladies at a table catty-corner from our table. He got the waitress' attention and pointed to the table and asked the waitress to give their bill to him. She smiled and did so.

As we were leaving and passed by the ladies table, I just wished them a wonderful day. We smiled and went to the register to pay. As we were at the register, I turned and saw a lady who looked just like my mom. My mom passed away in 2017. Bill saw her also and said the same thing. When he saw my tears, he already knew. Wow, who would have thought breakfast at Denny's could be so touching?

Now we are heading toward our destination, Rock Lake. We came across unique rock formations of all sizes. They were pretty interesting looking. They were a result of lava rock many years ago. On the same road, there were lots of wheat fields and hay. We saw a ring-necked pheasant running across the road. There were flat plains as far as the eye could see.

The rolling hills were a sight. There was no end. They rolled on and on forever, it seemed. Nature is so awesome. Driving through the quiet not so traveled road was peaceful. There was so much to observe. Usually, I have a lot to say, but today, I was almost speechless. We finally saw the sign we were looking for. I saw the excitement on Bill's face.

The weather was cold, cloudy, and overcast. It was coat weather. Even so, it was still a great day. My hands were really cold. It looked like it really wanted to rain on us. The first thing I noticed was a big dog taking a little human for a walk. It was so cute. There were several people fishing off the shore. Bill couldn't get out of the truck fast enough. Actually, I forgot Bill could move so fast (ha ha).

The gentle rippling water was serene and calm. It was tranquil just to sit and enjoy the scenery. Even though we didn't see any, we heard a small flock of geese. We met a nice couple fishing offshore. She was sitting in her chair, painting, and he was fishing. We had an instant connection. They invited us to stay for lunch. We visited and had a wonderful day at the new fishing spot.

16

Wake Up Our Senses

It's so refreshing to see the rain gently fall. The sound of falling rain is tranquil and soothing. The smell of the rain is clean and purifying. The rain has a way of waking up nature's senses and giving new life to spring. Soon we'll start seeing beautiful colored flowers, green lawns, and weeds in abundance.

Like us, our senses need to be brought to life from time to time. I think sometimes we forget. We are such creatures of habit and set in our ways we occasionally need to be reminded. Wake up to a new refreshing outlook on life. It can be a real eye-opener.

See the beauty that surrounds us every day. Hear the sounds of those who need a burst of sunshine in their hearts. By spreading happiness to those around us, we can make a difference. Our genuine efforts are never too small. They can have a domino effect on those around us.

This time of year is so amazing. I love going on walks and taking our little dog, Rocket. I can't help but to smile when I see how excited he gets when I get his leash. He starts jumping around like a little kangaroo. So adorable. Sometimes, I wonder who's walking who! He is such a joy to our family. It amazes me how something so small can have such a big impact on our lives.

Small acts of kindness, a smile, a hug, a "thinking of you" card—you get the picture. You don't have to do elaborate things to touch someone's heart as long as these things are done for the right reasons. We do these things because we want to, not because we have to. Nobody is telling us to act on the promptings we get. Our hearts tell us a lot if we only listen. Life has a way of sending us messages that we are not even aware of. Why do you think we're sent these messages? Maybe so we can grow and appreciate unexpected surprises, maybe just to be thankful for and recognize a blessing. What do you think? I don't think there is a right or wrong answer as long as we act.

We only have control over our actions. So let's make our actions come from our hearts. Do the *best* we can do to lighten someone else's burdens so they can feel our love. Who is on your mind to help ease their burdens? Pick up the phone and give them a call or drop by with a small gift. The possibilities are endless. Let your creativity flow and have fun with it.

17

Who Am I?

Sometimes that's a question that goes through all of our minds. Why am I here? Do I have a purpose? Who am I? Do I matter? We are so hard on ourselves. You do realize we are our worst critics, right? Let's put some light on those dark observations.

- You are here to be an inspiration to those around you.
- Your purpose is to make those you come in contact with feel your love and compassion.
- You are an important piece to life's puzzle. Without you, a special piece would be missing. We all somehow fit in the equation of life. It takes us all to complete God's perfect plan.
- At times, we treat ourselves unfairly. We don't give ourselves the respect we deserve.

Why am I here?

I am here to make a difference in society. Bring back courtesy, respect, politeness, and consideration. Whatever happened to opening the door for someone, saying please and thank you, smiling and making a genuine conversation?

Do I have a purpose?

Our purpose is to encourage those who need a helping hand. Gently guide them to move forward, try again and again if necessary. Let them feel our love and compassion. It is fun and rewarding to see someone improve their life and be happy.

Do I matter?

Yes. Absolutely. We all have something unique to offer. We all have strengths and weaknesses. By sharing our talents, we can give each other valuable ideas to get creative with our efforts to do acts of kindness.

Who am I?

At times, we don't feel adequate enough to accomplish important tasks. These are the times we need to step up and change the low self-esteem attitude we have of ourselves. You are a child of God, strong and courageous. That's who you are. You have a beautiful spirit. There is a fun, loving, compassionate side of you that wants to be put to use. Someone out there needs you. If we look for opportunities, listen for the promptings, and act when we feel the Spirit. We can do a lot of good in these troubled times.

I love this quote by Thomas S. Monson: "Some of you may be shy by nature or consider yourself inadequate to respond affirmatively to reaching out to others. Remember that this work is not yours and mine alone. It is the Lord's work, and when we are on the Lord's errand, we are entitled to the Lord's help. Remember That whom the Lord calls, the Lord qualifies."

18

Buddy

Buddy has been part of our family for over seven years. He is part border collie and part German shepherd. Did I mention he is a big dog? So playful and loveable. At first, I have to admit, I was a little intimidated by him. Little by little, I made an effort to get to know him.

He was always in the backyard, and I would see him play with our smaller dog, Rocket.

I figured if Rocket wasn't afraid of Buddy, I shouldn't be either. I started gradually going out back to get more acquainted with him. He was strong at playing tug-of-war. He liked to run and catch toys I would throw to him. Watching he and Rocket play was very entertaining. After a while, I grew to love them both. Somehow, now, they are both inside dogs. Go figure.

Buddy is my son Sheldon's dog. He takes him hiking and on daily walks when he gets home from work. He's a good obedient dog. Not to mention he is absolutely beautiful. The dogs enjoy camping and the great outdoors as much as we do. It's fun just to observe them getting rough and aggressive and then totally mellowing out. Rocket and Buddy have so much character. I'll tell them to "go get your toys." They get excited because they know you're going to play with them. I wonder what they would say if they could talk to us. That's okay, they speak, and we understand.

Rocket is an ornery four-year-old most of the time. I think Buddy tolerates Rocket's annoying behavior because he doesn't want to hurt him. Rocket's a lot more playful than Buddy is. There is a definite love-play relationship between them. Buddy has a deep powerful bark. Then there's Rocket with his yippee soft bark. It's funny to hear them both.

I hope you enjoy hearing about our family dogs. After all, they are part of our family.

ABOUT THE AUTHOR

This collection of her thoughts, outlook, and dreams is a true reflection of Pamala. Like many people, finding the good and positive in the little things sometimes gets overlooked, but this is a reminder that you can find good and the grace of GOD in everyday life. Pamala enjoys being with her family, scrapbooking, and vacationing with her husband, Bill. Pamala has not had the picture-perfect life, but she has not let her past define her future—actually, the exact opposite. She creates memories that show the positive effect we can have on others by just being a good person and lending a helping hand or maybe even a shoulder. I am lucky to be able to call her mom.

—Sheila Farmer (Pamala's daughter)